Living Abundantly

Manifestations of God and Giggles

Sandhya Malur

BookLeaf
Publishing

India | USA | UK

Made with ❤ on the BookLeaf Publishing Platform
www.bookleafpub.in
www.bookleafpub.com

Dedication

A friend gave me a great present for my birthday.
The plaque reads: "Live a good Story",
I love that.
Each of us has an interesting life story.
Live it, enhance it, let it unfold.
Let us Be Joy, let us Be Hope, let our Lives Sing.
Let it sing in Joy, Freedom, and Abundance!

I can feel the exuberance
creeping up in my soul at those words.
Corners of my mouth curve up.
My face and forehead relax.
Live a Good Story – let it sing, and move, and undulate.
Let it FLOW.
To Live in Flow is to live in Abundance.
Flow, that feeling of expansiveness,
where I am so immersed in what I am creating
fully absorbed by it.
Definitely "out of my head" for hours at a stretch.

So necessary for my analytical brain.
My questioning, curious mind
has made an excellent researcher.

Brought me a very successful career as an analytic
competitive research marketeer.
But life is about balance.
I bring forth a different kind of creativity
more visual and feeling based.
I feel the movement in my body, heart, and mind
through dance, yoga, walking, art, and writing
I create.

The Zen of Creativity is in the Flow.
Expanding, creative, joyful, hopeful, abundant.
Life is about creating,
trying new things, exploring the story.
Explore creativity.
Let go of perfectionism, of worry of how it will be
received.
Just create in joy. Enjoy.
Be In Joy, be In Hope, be In Flow Let your Life Sing.
Health, Wealth, Tranquility,
make for a full life.
In Joy, In Hope, In Flow, In Abundance.
Live a good story, grow your abundance.
In that spirit, I'm sharing my flow of creations with you.

Artwork and poetry by Sandhya Malur

Preface

Acknowledgements

Acknowledgement

Your support for my creative endeavors
So critical, wanted, needed....
You know who you are
Always appreciative, truthful
Acceptance of me as I am
Thank you, Thank you.
Feelings, meditative, spiritual

Beyond the confines of ordinary language
Lies my feelings
My thoughts....
Expressiveness....
Sitting at the lake
I hear the loons
Mate calling to mate
I understand.......
Beyond the confines of ordinary language
Heart music feeling the beat in your body
Evocative and imaginative

1. Meditative Walk

One day the clouds broke and the sun shone through.
Golden rays bringing warmth and light.
The yellow red of the trees......the fallen leaves
rustled beneath my feet as I walked.

I walked in the woods, the silky sun on my skin,
warm tones behind my eyelids.
I listened to the silence. It seeped,
into my brain and down my body.

Soothed my mind.... I meditate.
I walk. My mind expands, I have to silence my
thoughts.
It took two hours of fighting the chatter,
focusing on nothing.

To walk in silence.
To allow the pure thoughts to bubble up.
To hear my own voice in the stillness.
To feel the warmth inside and out.

2. Wisdom through the Silence in the Forest

The Silence in the forest
Listening to the silence
Watching nature, watching me.

Meditation brings Peace
It's a different feel from being in solitude
Inside. Meditating.

It's FULL. The trees speak to me.
The sun comes through the forest
Dappled at my feet.

I can feel it on my face
My skin sometimes - that warmth
I feel Safe.

Walking in the silence in the forest
I breathe deep. Let it out with a sigh.
What is the message? I listen. I hear. The Wisdom.

Maybe it's my own inner voice
God's guidance
Coming through the trees in the forest.

3. Listening, Dancing Love

When someone deeply listens to me
I am filled with hope, sunlight, a fresh breeze.
I stretch, I can grow, I love.

I dance, twirl, hear the music
Feel the summer breeze. See the light.
In my minds eye, I am open to creative.

I rise, I sway, I dance.
I am important, I matter.

When someone deeply listens to you
You are important, you matter.

Inspiration, expansion, joy, peace.
Energized excitement.

The listening love I give you is second hand, I got to feel
it first.

4. The Hub

The hub of a house that makes it a home is the kitchen.
We're in the kitchen crowded around the island,
the lights and shape of each piece lovingly chosen.

It's the food, the recipes handed down
from mothers and grandmothers

And also memories of the father
that taught me how to cook.

No real measurements – ever, but a process
to be ingrained.

A systematic, engineering approach of spices, in order of
use
laid out in the lids of the jars.......

Music, a glass of wine savored
lots of taste testing, a little dancing, singing....

Room needed for the activities and the bodies
was taken into account in the kitchen remodel.

The colors and the light
emanating warmth and welcome.

Melding spicy Indian foods into American fare
makes for the smells and sounds of happy eating.
The hub of a house that makes it a home is the kitchen.

5. Belonging

Am I IN or Am I OUT?
Are you letting me into "the club"? the group? the gang?

Can I feel at HOME?
As if in MY SPACE.

MY feel, MY Persona
No explanations required.

Uncertainty makes me aloof
A cloak of protection needed.

Until I come into my OWN
I fight, restless, prickly, cautious.

Until external shell turns
into inner strength, SOLID.

Of knowing, of BEING......relax
friendly, open, sharing.

Like the Caged Bird Singing
I let go, soar, fly free.

Glide on the wings of Life
Of Safety, Of Joy, Of ME.

6. Sparkles

Sun glistening on lakes.
Sparkles like firefly lights.
Diamonds rippling.
Glimmers of sunbursts.
Hope and Light in a frustrating world.

7. The Perfect Moment

Is space in my brain and in my heart.
Inhaling an aromatic cup of tea.
Feeling the hot liquid course down my throat.
Listening to a loon....
DEEP inhale, EYES CLOSED, EXHALE through pursed
lips.
It's warm, it's safe.
Bright and shiny.
Slight breeze on my face.
At ease, in comfort.
I look around, breathe deep,
content, with a sigh,
I thank God
for the Perfect Moment.

8. Loneliness

Loneliness is a sad gnawing feeling.
Drab, dark,
bred in sullen silence.
Lack of companionship.

Being alone
is a choice.
Joyful and freeing!

Joy comes when I chose it!
Introverted
I can be content
in my aloneness.

Dance, music, art,
reading, creating,
fill my soul.

And yes, a million friendships
give me the laughter and companionship

I need.

Serenity comes floating from the joy
from companiable silence.
Sometimes the silence speaks volumes.

I listen to the silence
to the voice of God
and I am not lonely.

9. Dream On

I dream on
across the sands of Time.
Chance has been in the wind
I have sweet dreams
in my crowded heart.

I feel safe
when I feel the wonder of it.
How fast your sting, jaded
down a one-way view of life

You may have hit a bottom
I don't remember.
I wish for laughter.

I felt I was in sweet pastures
I will rise, I hope,
I am breathing, forever.

I dream on.

10. Acceptance

Of what is…. Chaos.
Mediocrity will improve over time
I Hope. Maybe.
Regardless, I accept
Enjoy the good
What is. What is to be.
Be content

No pretense. No build up.
No grasping for the perfect.
Keep dreaming big dreams
Visualizing. Manifesting.
But not yearning in lack
Be content

Let go of Lack
Let go of comparison
Let go of what should be
Let go of perfect.
Or even just great or desirable. Just Be.

Keep the dream, keep the vision
Be content

Shoulda, woulda, coulda
True enough. Choices made.
Live for today. Do my best.
Live Free. Live Rich. Live Happy.
Keep the dream
Be content

Accept the investment.
Of time. Of love. Of energy.
Appreciate the good
Let go of the not. Of the lack.
Keep the vision of hope
Keep the dream
Be content

Build or rebuild?
A new friendship
A new contentment
A new hope. A different kind of love.
Appreciate being looked after
Our own way of being.

Laugh, stay light, stay fun
Have fun. Stay engaged.

Invested. Interested.
A new friendship.... Stay steady.
Contentment. Heart smiles.

Giggle. Live Life.
Keep the dream.
Hold on to the dream
Be content
So, Blessed!

11. Free Inside

You know my feelings
in your arms.

Like Spring Tulips
rich lovely colors.

Like a dream vacation
a feather on the breath of God.

The wind on my back
tropical seasons,

I feel romantic and free inside.

12. Hope and Light!

Remember what childhood felt like?
Endless summers.... fun festivals.

Easy-Breezy!

No work or responsibilities,
or need to take care of home or family or others,
no expectations...just FUN.

I admire their endless enthusiasm
those fathers and mothers of yesteryear.

I am trying to maintain balance and just BE,
do the needful while holding onto my heart.
It's hard. This is the season of my loss

...but it is also the season of Fun and Lights – Fairy
Lights!
It is the season of HOPE.

I love the lights.
Their bright twinkling spark of hope.
I try to be the spark of hope, of fun, of comfort, of
strength. Solid.

I try to be open to God's voice, my own heart, and
others,
I try to skip through the season. Lighthearted.

Easy-Breezy!

13. Feel Me

I need to feel heard and understood,
deep in my soul and at my core.
Being closely looked at and cared for,
cherished is the feeling I crave.
How I feel when someone deeply listens to me.

The soul-to-soul conversation and connection is water to
my thirsty heart.

When someone deeply listens, it is an inherent
understanding of values and goals...
hearts and minds meeting and agreeing.
A vigorous nodding of the head....
smiles and mutual laughter heighten the closeness,
Listen, really listen, and hear me, understand me.

Feel me. Please.

14. Endless Summer

Deep Creek Lake,
manmade, somewhere in Maryland.
Handed off to our fathers,
a week off for the mothers.

We kids loved it. Lived in the "Dad" RV,
dads so relaxed – drinking, laughing.
Only instruction – "don't drown!"
Older ones in charge. Oh, to be In Charge at age 10!

Only meant we made up the rules for Marco-Polo in the
water!
A week of grilled food and sand castles,
brown skin even darker.
Teeth gleamed by the campfire at night.

As we shrieked at ghost stories, told with voices deep.
Falling asleep giggling,

dreaming of the next sun-filled day.
Luscious, endless summer.

15. Beauty and Order

Come,
Celebrate the silence with me.

Appreciate the Beauty and Order
of the garden.

The fragrance of the peonies
the yellow daffodils.
Dancing in the breeze

The colors of the asters,
the zinnias.

Celebrate the silence
in the woods.

The freedom of walking,
breeze rippling my hair
Th silence is loud.

Profound.
Settles my heart.

Appreciate the Beauty and Order of the Universe.
Listen for the voice of the Creator.
nspiration flows.

.

16. Purposeful Beauty

I am Life in its Beauty,
its Artistry, its Dance, its Order.
I am Peace, Stillness, Music, Movement.

I feel the music in my body,
And express it in my dance,
in my paintings, in my photos, in my words.

I am expressive and communicative,
I am free, soaring above, floating......
I am purposeful, helpful...I take action.

I am Creativity, Stillness, Peace, Beauty, Order, and
Purpose.

17. Seasons of Hope

The yard is coming alive,
after the winters hibernation.

Colors bursting forth, crocuses,
purple sightings through final winter snow.

Snow all gone, bright green grass,
yellow daffodils, cups swaying in the breeze.

Some double colored,
buttercup yellow, deep sun yellow, orangey salmon.

Splashes of color, of movement,
planted and springing forth in bunches.

Edged with bright green diagonal leaves,
steady through the Seasons.

A comforting reminder that all is,
still, alright with the world

18. Did You Know The Things I Miss? (Letter to my grandchild about the past)

Did you know that we had Forests in Town?
Swathes of green trees and walking trails
Right by the water's edge

It was more than the burnt landscape of today
I miss, walking on the trails, sun peeking through
I miss, walking on the beach, hearing waves crash

I miss, sitting by the lake, watching the sunrise
I miss cool breezes! Me, who loves the warmth!
It's true! But I miss feeling the cool of the shade

Of green trees of the forest, of ocean spray
I miss predictable seasons
I miss bouquets of garden flowers

I miss the blaze of the poppies in June

I miss the lake running high
Children and dogs splashing and laughing

Instead, we have hot sun-blazing, temperature too high,
intense....
Choking heat killing living things
Shimmering heat, draining, enervating

Did you know that we had forests in Town?

19. Simple Serenity

In the pandemic I discovered simplicity, silence, serenity.

I hibernated and I loved it.
There was fear, of course. Until, Halleluiah! I take the
vaccine, the booster.
But before that, there was hibernation and time spent on
my own.

I luxuriate in the time, day after day.
I read, dance, watch tv, text, play.
Look around as I hike and walk by myself.

I notice. I am not lonely, rather alone.

I see with new eyes, my vision expands. I feel joy in
simplicity, in sleep,
in stretching my body, in Home. I notice.......
The deer in the background of Fall colors. The beauty in
our backyard.

It has always been there – to be noticed.

A family of deer appear and I am home to notice,
I have time to run to my phone, take a picture. Exclaim!
Watch the deer play. Make a photo panel. I love being
Home.

20. Giggles

I've been thinking about joy and giggling.
The joy, the mirth, delighted mouth agape.

Eyes lit up. Giggles bursting forth.

Children run, jump, laugh and play.
............Giggling at every turn.

Enjoyment & abandon. How do we recapture that?

Running through sprinklers.
Absorbed in the moment.

Lollygagging.......Lounging.........

Pure contentment brings giggles.

21. No Regrets

We were not that tender, you and I,
I chose to be with you. I loved you.
Wait for the end with you
But don't wish it, don't rush it.

I waited over the years.
In airports, security lines, on planes.
20+ hours in a seat in the sky, I waited.
A strange comfort from familiarity gained.

In silence, in solitude,
Alone, I wait to ultimately get there.
To you, waiting for me.
Cross an ocean, navigate life, work, and time zones, by
myself.

I bring my creature comforts and pretty things. I make
my home away from home.
Keep your loneliness at bay. I choose to be with you day
after day.

Relive memories, scrolling through photos, our heads
together as never before.
English gone, an opportunity to practice Malayalam.

Try to bring comfort, a spark, a smile, a laugh
Be patient. Be still. Just wait. Just be. Get close.
What do you do for all those weeks?!
Nothing. Companionship, meld with her routine.

Just wait. Just be. How long can I sustain this? I want to,
I must.
Don't feel alone or abandoned,
Keep afloat. Don't go into free- fall! Re-center, I want
you to feel loved.
Stay present. I am with you. Just wait. Just be.

Stay alert – does she have what she needs?
My heart aches for you, I choose you.
Laughter, gentle touches, tenderness blossoms,
Becomes us.

Just wait. Just be. We got close.
Did I do it right? Make the right choices? Retire?? Life
on hold
Waiting with Appa first, then Amma – spread out over 6
years.
I made the choice. Just wait. Just be. I have no regrets.

22. Awakening

You had a megawatt smile, personality to match
Long braid flips, your quips
Vibrant, fun loving, great cook, so welcoming!
Talented, an actress well known

Winning awards
Soaked up the limelight
Showing the way for women behind you
Your sophistication shone through

Gorgeous six-yards, silk and cotton saris
Bead and gold necklaces to match
Ankle length hair
Chanel No. 5, scent in the air

Inimitable style
I admired you, loved you, wanted to please you
Perfectionist tendencies instilled
Self-doubt, never good enough. Be better

Talent, zest, connection, artistry hidden amongst the
petals
all absorbed from you
Awakening to realize my own sweet flowering
I'm more like you than you or I ever knew

You saw I was there
Walls crumbled
I whispered, "I love you, all is well"
You slipped away, that last morning

23. Promises Kept

My body draped across yours,
the last time I saw you.
You asked me to stay - I could not.
Shattered, how I wished it different.

I whispered goodbye, my love in your ear,
your work here is done.
We'll look after Amma.
If you are ready, you can go.

You could go?! I was wracked,
permission to be free.
Only 2 months in bed – seemed an eternity.
Sun on my face, journaling and just watching.

I loved you,
singing, reciting Sanskrit prayers.
Taught by you in years gone by.
Was it the wrong thing to say? I wasn't wishing you
gone.

No longer the vibrant man of action, laughing and
singing,
body wracked by Parkinson's.
The one in a million – limbs get rigid kind.
Of course. That was you - one in a million.

I waited with Amma,
just as I did with you.
I whispered my love to her too.
I kept my promise.

24. Days gone by...

Up at the lake with her for the weekend.
Brings a sweet smile to her face
A smile of recognition? Joyful!
Wonderment, enjoying the vista
She says "it's a good view"!

Memories of yesteryear, days gone by......
A husband no more
Four young boys, grown men now
"Where is everybody?", she asks
Living back in time.

96 is a long life, a full life
Grateful for the good times
Used to be a quilting queen
A mile high apple pie maker
Sewer, clothes designer.

Creative, appreciative, faithful
God grant me the Serenity....

A woman of her time
Slowing down now, things take longer
Do you need help? Pride precludes it.

Still grateful, doing puzzles, a walk down the dock,
telling of stories.............
getting locked out and climbing in through windows
how "the camp" became a house, bigger, fancier.
Do you recognize the streets? The lake? Are you
comfortable?

25. What Is Happening?!

What is Happening?!

They say ANGER held in can turn
into depression and sadness and body pain.
I feel that. But I also feel RAGE.
So much shock that people seem not
to want or to even CARE to follow any rules or norms.
Won't stick to agreements,
act like sane grownups. What is Happening?!

What is happening in this world that
we cannot trust people to do the right thing?
What is happening in this world that people
act like thugs, crooks - that they have no self-control?
What is happening in this world that
everything is at the tipping point.
Boils over rage, hate, sadness, chaos, cynicism.

How do we bring back peace, fun, and ease?
How do we bring back simple decency?!

Let alone trust, love, and good-feeling?
What is Happening?!
I try to hold on to hope and light
Joy........
But it is HARD.

26. Someday Soon

Someday soon things will be easy and bright
tripping, skipping, delighted, free, and light.

I'll be practiced again in throwing my arms open wide,
come close to give and receive hugs, love, smiles side to
side.

Someday soon the world will be open and inviting,
welcoming me to explore, savoring, and sighting.

Enjoy the adventures, the people, the Bloom of Life,
free of strife.

Someday soon plans will be made, easily, snappily,
we will welcome all friends. BBQ in the sun, happily.

Laughter, joy, and freedom spilling,
sharing food, left open on tables, thrilling.

Someday soon I'll see your face and you'll see mine.

We'll smile, laugh, share joy, hugs, and souls will shine.

Someday soon the world will bloom,
Someday soon.

Please God.
Someday soon.

27. Resilience

We used to ask
What if the World shut down
and I finally had time?!

Now we know – COVID.
The Good, the Bad, the PTSD.

What If we focused on introspection and inspiration
rather than PTSD and isolation?

What if we focused on the joy, the learning,
the growth and fun?

Fulfillment, learning to be enough on our own
It is Strength and Joy and Fortitude shone.

It's Resilience.

28. After the Great Pause

It happened.
The Great Pause.
The World stopped.

Scary, yes...but,
the greatest gift.
Not the virus or the deaths.
But the opportunity to reset.

For reflection.
For reevaluation.
For clarity.

Bring back only what works.
Be mindful.
Be judicious.
Be careful.

Feel our feelings.
Luxuriate in the spaciousness.

Quantity of time not quality, limited.

Oh! the caring, the creativity!
Enjoy the outdoors,
feel the silky sun.
Breathe the sweet, clean air.

Choose wisely, stingily
What we watch.
What we read.
What we let back in.

29. Zen of Creativity

Life on hold in fits and starts
Nervous about people, viruses, outcomes.
This has become the rhythm of my days.
Can I change this? Do I want to?

It is hard
I hesitate, I am cautious.
Homebody, enjoying my introverted-ness.
Be careful not to slide into depression, into nothingness.

Be selective in my travel
Explore internally, carefully.
My creative journey.
Expands my heart and soul.

Expands my mind
Expands my days.
Let go of perfectionism.
Expand creativity. Expand hope. Expand joy.

30. Just Nice?

Barbie in a psychedelic, hot pink, neon green swirled
colored dress
High heels, pink plastic,
Earrings, diagonal darts to match
I spend my day behind the tree
My favorite, private hideaway
Sewing, making accessories, a scarf draped glamorously
A hot pink purse......
Flushed, presented with care
Received too casually, oh, that's nice, she said
Falling flat...oh, that's nice?

31. Love Blooms

I want to see the kitten transformed into a lioness,
when I look in the mirror.

Am I good enough? Do I do enough?
With intention and attention,
I hope, I grow, I create.

Blossom, petals reach out, skyward
Soaking up God's light....
love...support...confidence.

I smile at my reflection,
warm, fragrant scent arises in the senses of my brain.
Hello you! I know you!

Welcome.
Bloom, here in the light.

32. Burning for Space

Letting go of expectations
Mine and others.........the striving
The worldly definition of success

And accomplishments.

What is "success", an accomplishment?
I re-frame it, in my own worldview and values
Let go of people pleasing......Trying to please and make
smooth

De-clutter, Let it go, BURN IT!!!

Watch the small blaze ....the ashes floating away
Cleanse my heart, my mind, my environment
Make space for the NEW

Sit and do NOTHING.
Luxuriate, Read, Watch TV, Think, Just BE
What?! Nothing?!!

Do NOTHING?!!

The accomplishment is in the Doing of NOTHING, of
ALLOWING.
Just BE!
It's big for me

I need the Burning Ceremony.

My accomplishment, my "body of work"
Allowing creativity and joy – affirmative writing,
dancing, art
Space for expansiveness and joy

It's all ART and ACCOMPLISHMENT

Teaching, sharing.........a ripple of hope, one person at a
time.

Space..........the Wellspring of Hope, of Creativity, of Joy,
of Inner Peace, of Art....and Accomplishment.

33. What's Next?

I try to show up.
Taking a risk, I show up.
Rainbows, colors, twirling, creating,
.... excited to share.
Share the joy, the laughter, the wisdom,
...........................and then they ask.

What's it for? What's Next?

34. Making Space

DECLUTTERING!
Seems like my Life's anthem lately.
My mantra, Marie Kondo it!

I want to make physical space.
Leads to mental brain space.
Leads to soaring heart space.
Serenity and control and inspiration.
Expansiveness! Space!

Spacious rooms, spacious heart,
Clean, spacious, welcoming, warm life.
I long for it.

I welcome it
Welcome the peace.
Welcome the inspiration.
But first,
I must make SPACE!
HOLD IT! FEEL IT! READ IT!

Does it SPEAK to me? Does it make my heart SING?!

Overwhelmed by the paper
By the email Inbox, by clothes.
TOO MUCH STUFF!!!

35. Hope Rises

Hope rises on the horizon.
Sun coming up, my heart expands.

I listen to the secrets whispered in the morning breeze,
soft on my skin.

It's a new day dawning.
I turn my face up to receive the kisses of the warm rays.

A loon cries in the distance, sharing its song,
I smile.

I listen to God's voice,
as Hope Rises in my heart, in the morn.